"Penny Guisinger uses her 'postcards' to beautiful effect, not writing home from places in the world, but writing to the world from home. Which is at once a locale—rural, rough, and intimately known from mailbox to mailbox—and a state of mind, of soul. There really is a life compression going on here, with enormous quantities of felt (and endured, and devoured) experience getting compressed into wry, sorrowful, lyric communiqués from home to the world. Guisinger runs the table here, and we wait for the next rack…"
Sven Birkerts, author of *The Other Walk*

"*Postcards from Here* is completely captivating. Guisinger's precise prose, droll wit, and resonant voice offer us intimate, honest glimpses into love, parenting, survival, and earthy, everyday life as lived in rural Maine."
Dinty W. Moore, author of *Between Panic & Desire*

"Out of a remote corner of Downeast Maine comes a voice so quirky and compelling, we wonder how we've managed for so long without it. In *Postcards from Here*, Penny Guisinger has gathered pick-up trucks and orchestras, porcupines, pain, and pills for pain, coastal coves and moments from the sweet chaos of marriage. Each of these vignettes is filtered through a lyric sensibility and delivered with a keen eye for the perverse and the practical. Guisinger gives us what we go to literature for: the universal and often unspoken truths of our lives. What a breathtaking debut."
Barbara Hurd, author of *Listening to the Savage: River Notes and Half-Heard Melodies*

"Penny Guisinger's *Postcards from Here* has its hands deep in the plain rich soil of small town Maine life, with intimate, lyric particulars of hauling wood, parenting in the wake of divorce, the death of a neighbor, the way we shift with the seasons. It also digs at less expected terrain—love at the moment when same-sex marriage is made legal, and the ongoing battles against addiction. In a place full of hunters and prey, these micro-essays wear blaze orange: Guisinger's prose is alert and alive, visible and vibrant."
Arielle Greenberg, author of *Locally Made Panties*

Postcards From Here
Copyright © 2016 Penny Guisinger
All rights reserved.

Print Edition
ISBN: 978-1-925417-05-0

Published by Vine Leaves Press 2016
Melbourne, Victoria, Australia

Cover photo by Gary Guisinger
Cover design by Jessica Bell
Interior design by Amie McCracken

National Library of Australia Cataloguing-in-Publication entry
Creator: Guisinger, Penny, author.
Title: Postcards from here / Penny Guisinger.
ISBN: 9781925417050 (paperback)
Subjects: Short stories.
Dewey Number: A823.4

a memoir in vignettes

Penny Guisinger

Vine Leaves Press
Melbourne, Vic, Australia | Athens, Attica, Greece

Table of Contents

For Mom and Dad.
For Abby and Owen.
And for Kara.

(Also for the porcupines.)

I Didn't Miss You Until This Morning

I pushed aside leaves in the eggplant bed wishing we had grown just one. Plummy, earthy fruit that tastes like warmth, the floor of the forest, and chocolate. You love these plants with violet blossoms, their leaves interrupted by lines the colour of dusk. They bore nothing but beauty and form, but I suppose that's something. I did my work while you were gone. I slept hard, stayed sober, weeded. I hauled basil plants out of the earth and plucked them down to bare stems, lifted drooping tomato branches, pulled all the ready fruit. Sturdy kale, pumpkins, butternuts and buttercups. (I can never remember which is the nut and which is the cup, but I know you know.) By now, your tent was stuffed into its sack, the sack into a dry bag, and all of it afloat with you down a fat river under this same coastal sky. I was not irritated anymore. Who does the dishes, who calls the vet, who hangs the sheets out to dry. Trivia. I filled a whole, black enamel canner with tomatillos, sungolds, and slicers, then looked for more. There were so many mornings when I had my face in a book, fingers in some writing project. You were probably irritated with me, as you dug to reveal potatoes like gold nuggets. I was leaving the garden, carrying the bounty, when there, buried in the shin-high foliage—one eggplant, the size of a fist. I want to tell you.

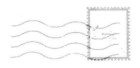

Sentry

The summer's heat is almost over. Yesterday, a flurry of yellow leaves descended on my car on a shady back road. We sleep deeply in dry evening air, no more unwelcome dampness in the sheets. I look forward to jeans and socks, to hot soups. The garden is birthing and birthing ripeness and more ripeness. We can hardly keep up preserving all this bounty. The freezer's supply of cherry pops and ice cream is dwindling to make room for bags of kale and green beans, pureed tomatillos. These are meals to come once the garden is covered in snow. The late afternoon light nudges closer to orange, and it paints the trunks of white pine and birch as the sun revolves down into the forest a little earlier each day. The tallest sunflower opened its great yellow eye yesterday.

Death of a Neighbour

The truck was parked next to their driveway. Something about its angle, the short distance between its radiator and the pine trees, suggested haste, but we went to bed because it was late and that's what people do. The next morning, we heard the news: Walter had died. It made my knees fold and I had to sit to take it in. Over the next days, while we handed these words back and forth between us—"So sudden. So young. So hard to believe,"—a chant moving through our town like the tide, I did not wonder how his wife felt. We think we know this. Instead I wondered what it's like to be a paramedic on call the night another paramedic, who was supposed to have the night off, goes down like that, so sudden. When the pager goes off and the news comes in and you speed in your pickup truck to his house, where your co-worker has already started a line, what do you say to the dying man on the gurney who is usually next to you, handing you a syringe? When he tries to make a weak joke, do you laugh? And what is it like to be Walter, to recognize the symptoms? Headache. Blurred vision. Sudden onset. Vomiting. Did he know? This speculation is mine, but also everyone's. We try to shovel in the gaps the way we move snow, clear out the blanks.

At the funeral, in the cavernous school gymnasium, uniformed first responders took up the first five rows of metal folding chairs. They stood, in unison, volumes on walkie talkies turned to ten, while dispatch paged our neighbour. Once. Twice. Final call. No one answered. No one sat down.

Postcards from Here

11

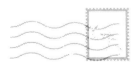

Off My Meds

This body is a standard, and I'm used to automatic shifting between speeds, between textures. I don't like the space between movements, that hanging pause of nothingness when I move the stick. The vehicle responds all wrong. Steering across the bearings is so stiff when I'm used to the power kind, and it's too much work to roll the windows up and down by hand, cranking that little handle around and around. It might break off in my grasp. The mirror's adhesive has let go, leaving this rectangle of reflection in my lap. It shows me nothing but my own knees. I am not on them. Shredded rubber blades hang from the wiper arms. Messy. Not even the roads are the same. The familiar drive to work is misty and vague, turns in the road arching the wrong directions. But I am a hard driver to kill. I've seen all those trucker movies, and I know my handle and how to press the pedal. I know my own mettle. I am studded snow tires in a blizzard—in chains. I can drive this.

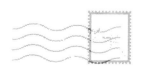

Batboy is Disappointed

I assemble the Batman costume. He wants black gloves, and can only find one. He can't find the dark knight's utility belt either—anywhere. I tell him that I'll look for the glove, but sometimes things get lost. I want to tell him that we lose years too, under the furniture and in pockets of the coats we outgrow. I'm shining a flashlight under the couch when he says, "Why don't you keep track of these things?" I can't find the belt. Or the glove. I give him my black gloves, and he scowls at the furry, green stripe on each wrist. "Batman doesn't wear green." His mouth becomes a hyphen underneath bat ears and mask, and silky cape billows behind him as he darkly menaces up stairs covered in beige carpet. I move the couch, looking for the years, trying to keep track.

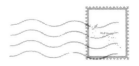

Valentine's Day

Her scarf draped around her neck, exposing her ear and earring. That supple glimpse held my attention through the kitchen window while she pushed snow off the windshield of my Honda, just leaving for work, nothing special, but totally special because she was driving my car instead of hers. My standard shift, five-speed that she had learned to drive when I couldn't because of this stupid shoulder surgery that I would recover from, but not for a while. It was the season of record-breaking snowfall, and I was off shovel detail and most firewood detail and had to drive her automatic transmission most of the winter. I lifted a steaming coffee cup to my lips, watching her whisk snow off the hood with a wooden-handled brush, and I thought about marriage and the new ardor that settles in after years together—the sexiness of domesticity, of standard comforts and help. I wanted her to come back inside and let me untwine her scarf and her clothing and to make love in the living room like we used to when we were new and I wrote an entire poem about her shoulder. But she had to be in her classroom in a few minutes and I was writing on a deadline, and so I drank coffee and watched her toss her computer bag in the back seat of my Honda, climb in, and drive away.

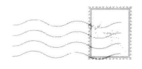

Guns and Beer

On my way home at lunchtime to fill the woodstove and let the dog out, my car crests a hill, and I come across two pickup trucks by the roadside and two men standing next to them. To say the trucks were "parked" there suggests a more orderly arrangement than the one I came across. If not for the presence of the men, one of whom was holding a rifle and the other a Bud Light can, it would have been easy to assume that the trucks had been abandoned there in a moment of fright. I stopped my car, and eased my window down. "What's up?" I got the story. They were hunting coyotes. "Why on earth are you doing that?" Earnest expressions, like they had been caught by the teacher. They're bad for the deer herd, don't you know? We came to help Bernard, cuz he killed one, but he just wounded the other'n and it got away. We came to help him find it and he gave me this beer. "I live at the end of this road and we've got little kids that live back there. I don't want a bunch of gunfire." Oh no, ma'am. We're very careful. A slight lift of the beer can offered to emphasize the sincerity of the caution.

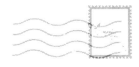

New Normal

I took them to school on a Friday morning, knowing that their dad would pick them up to take them to his parents' house for the weekend. We expect it, these days. One parent drops off, the other picks up, and the parents don't live together anymore. It used to be lobster bakes and wine for me too on these weekends with his parents. Patti made bowls of spicy-mean crab dip. Dana poured stiff vodka tonics on the rocks, with lime slices suspended like jewels in the bubbles. I picked leaves of mint and oregano from the herb garden Patti planted in the raised bed, edged with rocks. Lingering until too late in the afternoon on Sunday, we arrived home to carry sleeping kids into our glowing house. That Friday morning, I flipped the mirror up so the kids couldn't see my wet eyes. My son sighed, breaking his own reverie, "There are so many reasons I wish I had a time machine."

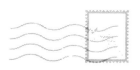

Back from the Trip

And so you come home after a week-long trip—not even a week. Just gone four nights, you return with a backpack over your shoulder, the scent of skiing and wood smoke and sleeping bags on your red flannel. You return to wine and candlelight and our song playing and stir fry with peanut sauce over quinoa. Locally-made tempeh. Steaming grains. I know this feeling. You have been travelling and are not ready for the romance I have planned. You need a minute and a shower. I fill the wood stove, give you the time. Then, when the quinoa is gone and we have relaxed by the fire and filled each other in on the events of the past five days, you are ready. And now I am tired from the wine and the wood stove's heat and the anticipation. And so I need a minute and a night's sleep to get where you are. And so in the morning, when I come to you with coffee and lock the bedroom door and reach up your t-shirt, you manage to be surprised.

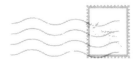

Tourist Town

We're at the table by the window, which doesn't say much since the whole place is windows. We're close to the front—facing the street—just in from the sidewalk. Beyond that, is the other summer tavern across the street and beyond that is the bay. Seals bob for fish in the current, and we're surrounded by tourists. Just three days before Labor Day. Three days until the busyness eases and the work days get shorter. Our waitress is hustling—five full tables, people from New York and Massachusetts—they are never quite happy. Outside, a truck has slowed. A small arm, baby fat just fading from the wrist and elbow, extends through the window, reaching toward the restaurant. The waitress sees it too, and lifts her own hand in acknowledgement, a small smile appears then fades as another order is ready. Another plate of fish and chips. Another pint. The truck slowly moves past, and the small hand keeps waving like a flag.

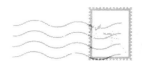

Calligraphy

Katie sits in our living room, writing on rocks she brought with her. They're smooth, round beach rocks with flat surfaces. This is her new hobby—writing words on rocks. In between telling us the details of the conversation in which her marriage ended, she copies symbols from a book of lettering with green and blue calligraphy pens. Then she cries some more. She tells us that "b" and "y" are hard to write, and that she looked her wife straight in the face and said, "It's over." I ask her what she does with the rocks. She puts them on windowsills, fills bowls to the brim with them, gives them to people, returns them to the beach. There wasn't much to say after the words "I don't love you anymore" were spoken, so her wife packed a few things and drove away. "Imagine," she says to me, "walking along the beach and finding a rock with a word on it."

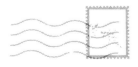

Hay Pond

We gather by that northern pond for the weekend. Scrambling eggs with chanterelles, these men play banjos, write poems, carry babies under their arms while they sing perfect harmony and drink coffee. These men chop wood, change tires, earn their livings, till soil, play mandolins. With beards and plaid shirts, they look women in the eye, not the chest, when they ask with interest how you are and how you slept and would you like more coffee. Laughing at late-night exploits (something about finding the bottom of the keg) not bragging, but sheepish, smiling, they compare who drank what, and they welcome the women's gentle teasing. They absorb it into their skin, while they scramble eggs by the pond. Sepp hears us singing in the living room, and asks nobody in particular if they hear that heavenly sound. It rains all weekend, and we accept it as permission to read books, play cards, learn new chords. We hear coffee mugs being set on tables, cast iron skillets being scrubbed, softly hissing gas lamps burning light, and rain against the windows. Someone picks up a fiddle.

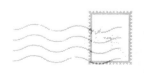

Defiant

The neighbours started calling when they heard. "Are you guys okay? Do you need to come over?" Offers of loaners came down our long snowy road. "We have an extra. Do you want to borrow it?" While more snow fell than had ever fallen before and temperatures broke every January record, we strategized like generals how to move a five-hundred-pound wood stove off a truck and into the house. How do you perform that Promethean act when the snow is higher than your hips and the fire weighs as much as a piano? Our stove spent twenty-six years on a rectangle of soapstone performing the magic of being what it was: a box of fire in the living room. The air control lever broke at the beginning of the season; it just spun around under our fingers, connected to nothing, so we had controlled air (because we actually get to control air) by leaving the glass doors open or closing them or something in between. The grates inside rusted to dust and some piece on the back of the firebox crumbled along the bottom edge. When the damper jammed in the open position and let the fire lick the inside brick of the chimney, it was over. Winter took on a new darkness and chill. The thermostat controlling the back-up propane heat turned under our fingers, and we hid in the room with the warmest registers while the rest of the house went cold. But propane's heat is thin and watery, like a fluorescent bulb to someone used to yellow incandescence. When my father delivered his old Shenandoah, a hulking black dictator of a thing, we took off our socks and let its warmth permeate our toes and soles.

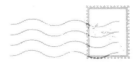

Donkey Sitter

"When you find a good donkey sitter," explains Beth, "you suck up." Owning donkeys makes it hard for Gary and Beth to travel, as does owning a book store, dogs, and a garden, but when they can, they get away. For this trip, they packed up copies of the famous writer's new novel so they could traverse the state, attend the reading, camp at the state park, and call it work. They sold books at the back of the room, and knew they didn't have to worry. They had cultivated their donkey sitter well, plying her with donkey-themed gifts from everywhere. Her daughter's first word was, "Donkey." Gary, with his long, gray beard and cranky political views, and Beth, with her colourful head scarf and round glasses, don't make it up to my part of Maine very often. Their store is four hours to our south. I have to imagine that, after they packed up their tent and were traveling home through our blueberry barrens, cobalt with heavy fruit, they imagined moving here with their donkeys, dogs, and garden. I would buy slim volumes of Gary's poetry, postcards of famous writers, and vegan cookbooks from the sale table. I would be their donkey sitter.

Penny Guisinger

22

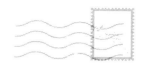

Fill in the Blank

My daughter attended the talk by the author who hiked the Appalachian Trail with his son, and now she's ready to hoist up a backpack and hit some summits. She knows this used to be my dream as well—abandoned to work and school and her. In the telling and the asking, she says that she wants to hike the *Application* Trail, and I hide my smile at her mistake. I have hiked that trail before, and will again, for work, for school, for her. Resumes like rocks and roots in the trail. Grad school selection like a narrow pass. Loans, mortgages, credit cards, state assistance, sliding scale fees at hospitals—mountain ranges of forms and ink. Triplicate at least. We balance, placing one boot carefully in front of the other along the thin edges of staples and blanks to fill in, hiking toward another day of hiking. Some day, I tell her. Some day you will hike the Application Trail.

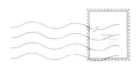

Red Cabbage

If Jackson Pollack could paint something on Stonehenge, it would remind me of red cabbage. Abstract art. Ancient rituals. Matter folded in and around and up against itself. So tightly coiled and packed. A cabbage seed is the size of a grasshopper's foot. From this miniscule packet, ancient codes unpack themselves. That seed chants to itself as it decants the DNA. It creates form above and below into soil and air. Not a fraction of a breath of space unused, the leaves pack tightly, fold in and around and up against each other, grow thicker or thinner as space allows or demands. Like looping spirals and stars growing in the white margins of a notebook. Each leaf lays down in just the right spot, and when they are pulled apart, unlocked from each other, they squeak. A sound like rubber against glass.

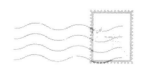

October into November

Grey stripe sunflowers in my garden stare heavily at their feet, like old people waiting in line for service, their faces ringed with shriveling yellow scarves. The Inuit have at least fifty words for snow. Surely, New Englanders must have at least that many for yellow and another thirty-six for the browns. The hay field, lit up like Van Gogh's last field of wheat before his suicide, is cornered by birch and tamarack in furious amber. Anything not yellow is brown, except for the blue, as the last greens are suctioned into our straw-covered field. The pea trellis, knee-deep in arugula and lettuce gone-by, wears a blue morning glory tucked behind its ear. And one of the sunflowers bends and nods to the flopping weight of an upside-down blue jay clinging to its face. The bird hangs there like a raven-ous azurite pendant.

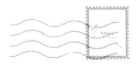

Grounding

Grounded in Detroit by the massive east coast blizzard, we took the shuttle bus to the Quality Inn and Suites for a handful of hours' sleep before Delta slipped us out in the early morning. Hungry and anxious, we craved food and beer. We found both across the snowy parking lot in the bar under the Day's Inn. With platters of veggie burgers and fat, greasy fries in front of us, surrounded by big screen football games, we listened to the table of young South Korean men try to place an order with our sharp, Midwestern waitress. She tried to tell them that one order of wings was not enough for all of them, then asked if it was North or South Korea that was the bad one. They were baffled by the small number of wings she brought them, then asked her to bring them her favourite. Young and slim and dark-haired and fun, she slid into a seat at our table, asking, "Can I get your opinion about something?" She had left her phone on the bar, and that drunk guy sitting over there—he's a regular—had answered it when it rang. "I was busy working," she said, twisting her hair. "What if that had been my mother or my boyfriend or something?" We affirmed. "Not cool." She rose, nodding. "I'm pissed. I've had it." She put in an order for a corned beef sandwich for the men from the good Korea.

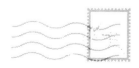

Essence of Cake

You are in the kitchen and I see my nine-year-old daughter, Abby, wander through. We are guests in the home of our old friends, and Abby has questions for them. *Do you like to cook?* She also has information. *I like to help Mama cook. I help her make cakes.* She eats a bowl of bean and kale soup and the simple health of that makes me proud—like I have done my job. She eats kale and reads books: it's all I have to give her. With a bath towel wrapped around her head, she looks like a spa patron, and she sings to the dog. She has just come out of a bergamot oil bath and she smells like wealth, like traces of citrus, like someone left fingerprints of plenty on her small body. I have not made her a cake in a while, and I usually don't let her help because it takes longer, and so I don't understand that weepy feeling when she says she likes to help me bake—like another thing I'm only appearing to get right. It's as if the memory of whatever cake we last baked is better than the cake itself. You offer to comb her hair.

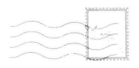

Letting The Terrorists Win

They came back from the playground talking about bullies. Two older boys, but not even older, just older-acting, telling them what to do and making up rules. "They said they were the police and that we had to pay them $500." I am surprised by the bitterness that rises up into my stomach at this story. Some old fear that I didn't remember I had. This campground seems, suddenly, like a bad neighbourhood. Last night's radio playing and slightly-too-loud laughter wafting over from another site seems ominous now, less innocent. My kids are in the camper, eating bagels, deciding whether these other boys qualify as bullies or not. "Bullies knock you over and take your lunch money." My kids have never carried lunch money. "That's them." My son points an accusing finger at two boys ambling past our pop-up. They hear him, and turn to face us. By the time I get the door open, they have fled. From me. Bullies have never fled from me. I am ready to talk to these boys' parents, but truly I have no idea what to say.

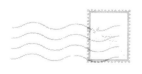

Love by the Numbers

Eight thousand volunteers collected over one hundred seven thousand signatures in support of our marriage. The campaign changed twelve thousand voters' minds with two hundred twenty five thousand conversations. We won with a six-point lead, and Maine became the eighth state to decide that men could marry men and women women. Four Portland bakeries donated over sixty wedding cakes to feed the seven hundred people who attended the victory banquet. All that data comes down to the heartbreaking way you pick up the pitcher and refill my water glass because you know I am thirsty. Your delicate wrist exposes itself to me as you place the pitcher next to the fifty-seventh wedding cake.

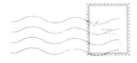

Whitetail

Outside my window, three white-tailed deer pick their way through blueberry barrens at the edge of the woods. Each wet hoof lifted and placed with the delicacy of blown glass. Swift-footed and unpredictable, these animals are not thinking about love's invisibility. That's my job. They graze, then lift their heads, synchronized so that at least one always has its attention on my back door. Their backs, slick with this spring rain, ears stick straight out like sails. Something changes, and the deer decide, as one mind, to ease into the tree line. Tenuous in their concealment, picking their way into the scrubby trees. It's as if they wrap themselves in cloaks of invisibility, like superheroes. They dissolve and fade, first into deer-shaped forms in the trees, then immediately nothing. From inside the trees, one deer flicks its tail, momentarily visible like a signal flag.

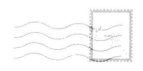

Concourse E, O'Hare

I find a tea shop at 7:30 am. To call it a tea shop suggests something more prim than the takeout where I bought yet another quart of coffee and something called a "black bean cheddar egg bite." The place is all greens and browns, leaf-themed with recyclable-looking cups and bags. It's laughable, really, because you can't recycle a disposable coffee cup in the airport or anywhere else, but I am a sucker for good packaging, and I'm hungry. Plus, unlike anyplace else in Chicago, I can eat here for less than the cash I have in my pocket. (This city finally coughs up a break in my direction when I have one foot on the tarmac.) The woman in front of me has ordered some complicated-looking combo of fruit and oatmeal and the container is handed to her with the cover askew. She asks for a bag. Her long, red fingernails make it impossible for her to fully grasp the container, bursting as it is with mango and other rainforest-inspired fruits. There are other things not graspable in this airport—this farce is only one of them. She can't keep the eco-friendly paperboard lid in place, and get it into the bag with the bamboo motif. The edge of the lid hooks on the handle of the bag making the bag collapse over and over. Strains of "We Will Rock You" waft across from the bar that is inexplicably open.

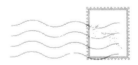

Marriage

My wife catches porcupines with the trash can and the lid the way you or I catch spiders with a glass and a piece of paper. Porcupines are bad neighbours. They let themselves into the garden, and take one bite out of every tomato, every squash, every cucumber. They climb up our ornamental trees and rip off the branches, leaving ugly holes near the top. We can't decide if they're brazen or just stupid, the way they ransack the place in daylight, with us standing right there. They know enough to run, though, when Kara bounds toward them with the trash can. I watched her one morning chase a fat porcupine clear across the grassy expanse of our lawn. It waddled as fast as it could, and Kara (wearing pajamas still) had to toss the bulbous, plastic trash barrel ahead of her to capture it. Her aim was good. The barrel landed on the fleeing animal just cleanly enough to halt its escape. I do not support porcupine relocation. I worry too much about babies being left behind or porcupine homesickness, but I have learned to stay out of this. From the porch, coffee in my hand, I watched her wrestle the trash can lid beneath the soft feet of the porcupine, then she rolled the whole package over, sliding the creature to the bottom. She stood next to the barrel, breathing hard, and asked me if I would get some rope from the garage. I hate that she loads them up and drives them down the road. Hate that they are scared and confused and lost—I project too much. I regard her there, in flannel pajamas and a T-shirt. Then I put down my cup, go to the garage, and get the rope.

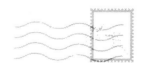

Marriage Two

He was a super model. A presidential candidate. A porn star. He stood in the field in front of our house, basking in his own light. The spectacle stopped me, quite literally, in my tracks. I had not seen this before, and it took several seconds for my brain to understand the information coming in over the retinal wire. He was as grand as he could make himself—feathers puffed out, almost standing on end, and tail opened like a fan. Not only standing, but slowly turning himself in place, to show every angle, every facet. He looked like he had walked right off the front of a Thanksgiving card from Hallmark, so perfect was his tom turkeyness. He wanted her to see. She was nearby, pecking at the grass, striding slowly away from him, wholly uninterested. Undaunted, he began to slowly move forward, as if he walked a thin catwalk, nodding to his fans. Aloof but aware. She was too busy to even glance at him, and that's when I noticed a slight motion near her long, still tail feathers. Then more. Then the motion took the shape of four gray puffballs that followed her in a perfect line. Babies. He had, clearly, impressed her at one time and now just wanted some of the romance back. She pecked and grazed, keeping one eye on the babies, training no eyes on him. She was done with him, maybe just wanted him to stop showing off and help keep track of the puffballs. He serenaded her with a burst of sound like gurgling water, shaking his wattle. Nothing. She turned away. The puffballs collected by her scaly, yellow feet. She was busy. The tom stopped his pivoting, lowered his feathers, and shrank. He transformed from the rock star to the guy who delivers our mail, the guy with the good job and the steady paycheck.

"I love you. Goodnight. Bye."

Staring into the ten-gallon tank of tropical fish, I call their dad's house. "Mommy, you're not calling at a very good time." Neon tetras school and unschool behind plastic plants. A wall of bubbles erupts from a wand buried under gravel. "I'm building a Lego robot guy." Reclining on the tweedy brown futon, watching the aquarium channel, I am drinking too much. Pry the cap off another local microbrew. As long as I'm counting the calories it's okay. "I was just calling you to say good night." Dark square behind me reveals yard and trees lit by the newly waning moon, and beyond that, coastline and farmland and neighbours tucking in their children or drinking their own beers or watching sports where someone actually wins. "Do you want to call me back?" Albino catfish drift into bubbles and get shot to the surface, then they do it again. Is this a game? "No, that's ok. I'll just say good night right now." Empty bottles on the coffee table next to my feet. I want just one more so I can sleep later. Behind me, the ocean rolls over in its sleep, following the moon whether it wants to or not. Bottle cap in my fingers, tapping it against my ring just for the tinny sound. Just for the contact.

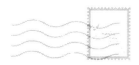

Refuge

I drive Nova Scotia, and you drive New Brunswick. We push across the five hundred miles of Sackville, Antigonish, Amherst, St. John, St. Andrews, St. Stephen. There are hotels, but we want to wake up in our own bed. I take back the wheel, then customs (where our cooler is searched), then Calais, then through the wildlife refuge to home. Across the final forty miles, my eyes struggle to stay open and both kids are asleep behind us and behind them, the dog is asleep too. Two out of the three are snoring, and the moonlight follows us down that dark road. I have to stay alert—any single dark shadow could be a moose waiting to leap in front of us, to destroy our radiator, our vacation, our lives. Your hand is on my knee and my hand is on the gearshift. Your eyes are on me and my eyes are on the road. "You can do this," you say, and I want to agree. The road lifts and drops us like a tide coming back to the beach.

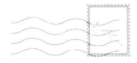

Buttery Light

The light this morning struck the snow on the trees outside our window, turning it to butter. It was the warmest light from the earliest sun in the coldest season. February, 7 a.m. light after a snowfall when the sun has just cleared the treetops and the colours are saturated with slate and cobalt and lemons. Colours so startling they interrupt my heartbeat, set my breathing on a new rhythm. Things are so still, and the coffee steams in my cup, and I am, just for a moment, aware of my own good luck—to live here, perched on the ocean's edge, watching that creamy light walk its way across the landscape with the whole day ahead. And I know there are at least five inches of hot coals downstairs in my woodstove, waiting for another stick of birch, and that makes me even luckier. This home accepts and creates warmth—sort of the way good luck invites more good luck—a momentum of light.

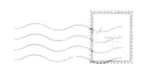

The Community Orchestra

Cocky young cello player in first chair might just fall asleep during the rest measures. Is he even counting? Two chairs back, a retiree has her fingers already in place. Her head bobs, her lips move, she is counting. One and two and three and four and. Stage right, the violin soloist shifts her weight from one foot to the other, hip cocked. Bow hanging off her finger, rest position, she uses her other hand to drape her long, black hair away from her bare shoulder, down her back, out of the way. Moments before she took the stage, those same fingers were flicking ash off the end of a lit cigarette in the church parking lot. The upper riser, behind and above the strings, is filled with brass and the other winds. Bassoon. Flute. Piccolo. The whole section capped with a lawn of grey curls and polished bald spots. Bows rise and fall like branches caught in a tide across a half acre of violins, flanked by an earnest young banjo player volunteering percussion for the night. In front, the conductor points in that certain way, with great urgency, at the section that's on the wrong measure.

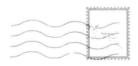

Torn Supraspinatus

"I'm an alcoholic," I told the surgeon. "And I'm nervous about the pain pills after the surgery." His button-down shirt was the colour of dark lilacs, his tie was blue, and he didn't know a goddamned thing about addiction. "Oh, most people don't even enjoy Oxycontin," he tried to assure me without sitting down. He was not tall, but from my seated position I had to tip my neck back to see his face. "Hopefully, you just won't like it as much as you liked alcohol." His hands were shoved into the pockets of his dark, blue chinos, and he looked directly into my eyes while I wondered if what I had felt toward my drug was anything like "like." He waited for my next question, and I thought of the opiate addicts in my town and whether they "liked" their drug the way we like oxygen, and then I was lost in the pondering of why these two substances shared a prefix. "Besides," he added, heading for the door, "we'll only send you home with enough for the first four weeks." Now that the booze was gone, and the nicotine, did he seriously think it would take upwards of thirty sunrises and sets for my sobered-up cells to find their way to this new thing? "It's not the same thing," he added. "It's completely different." I noted that he had not asked how many clean days I had behind me, and wondered if it mattered that it was fewer than thirty. Before he left, he said, "You have to do this, you know. You're not going to get any better without it."

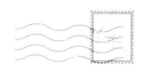

Don't Shoot

Around here, unless you dress yourself up like a traffic cone, you can die in your own driveway just for taking a walk. To go to our own mailbox, we sport a seasonal collection of hats, vests, and bandanas in a shade of orange called "I'm not a deer." In the eleventh month of every year, men tuck their big bellies behind the steering wheels of their big trucks and drive endlessly up and down our driveway and everyone else's. They're looking…just looking. They drive up and down all month. Gravel popping and snapping under the weight of their tires, often late enough in the morning that all the deer are long gone. They come all the way up to the house, and then slowly go back down to the road. Just looking. Some mornings, I meet one on my way to work on the narrow road, and I have to crowd the roadside bushes to keep our side panels from swapping paint. My wife and our dog and our kids and I do not venture any further than the corner of the garage without putting on our "not a deer" costumes. We are waiting for the safety of the twelfth month.

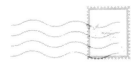

Curvature

Get backpacks. Find the permission slips for the field trip on Friday that their Dad forgot to send to my house. ("He forgot" is code for "he never looks through the piles of paper they bring home.") Remember gym shoes. Remember mittens. Drop off and keep driving. Go to the physical therapist's office to waste time learning minor exercises that won't help my back. Forget my phone. No, bring the phone, but forget that the battery is dead. ("I forgot" is code for "I can never find the charger.") Call my office anyway, from the dying phone, and tell the nice intern that I'll be late. He's new and says, "Ok. Who do you want me to tell?" The phone dies before I can instruct him on the obvious. The physical therapist is half my age and less than half my weight. She is that thing we call "perky," but I like her anyway because she lets me bring in my coffee. She says it's my spine that's twisted. That's my problem.

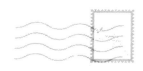

Tide Mill Farm

It would be faster if we had a boat, but we don't, so we drive around the cove to the farm. It's Saturday, and our farmer has her market open. Nobody works harder than Carly. There's a chair behind the cash register on the card table, but she's not in it. She's crouched, sorting carrots, by breed, into two wooden baskets. Ruth, the baby, is pasted to her front, held in place by a canvas carrier with the buckles cinched down. Silent and blond, youngest of four, Ruth is growing up in motion, carried through air thick with manure and sweet hay. Kara and I write a large check each spring that serves as admission to Saturday markets. We load up with whatever grew that week, and Carly writes it on our page in her fat spiral notebook, deducting the price of butternut squash, storage onions, or slick bags of cranberries from our slowly shrinking credit. She's got one hand on the pen, and with the other, works a walkie talkie, asking one of the interns to harvest more Brussels sprouts. Ruth hangs in place, pivoting her head around to look at us, and I make a goofy face to see if she will smile. She doesn't, but Carly does—Carly is, somehow, always smiling—and she asks us how we're doing and if we need anything else. Kara asks about beets. Next week, we're told, when there's been more time to ease them out of the earth. There's never enough time to milk the herd, pull the roots, slaughter and pluck the chickens and turkeys, homeschool the kids, deliver milk all across the county in the refrigerated truck they can barely afford to keep on the road, and gather eggs. She apologizes for not having beets, and we tell her it's really okay. We can wait.

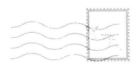

White Rain

The sky is beginning to lighten, and as it does, the rain becomes more visible, falling the way that it is, in sheets billowing in gusts of wind. The rain starts to reflect back opaque light, becoming more visible as the dawn turns into day. Then, so slowly that it's almost one at a time, the raindrops turn to snow. I sit in the privilege of watching this transition from the warmth and dryness of my desk, surrounded on three sides by huge windows. Against the backdrop of a forest so dark green that it's almost black, these raindrops yield their liquid form and become crystalline. First just a few. Then more. Then even more, until I am engulfed in white squall. Invisible against the white clouds, and vanishing when it strikes the warm ground, the snow lives its whole lifespan against this band of dark green. It is both intensely serious, in its speed and focus, and not, for its short life. The flurry lasts only minutes, then the clouds shift, the temperature adjusts, and one at a time, the flakes unfreeze back into water.

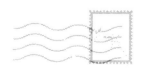

Free of the Water

The fish are out of their tank and swimming through the air in the hallway outside the dorm room. (Mandatory disclosure: this is a dream.) Bright orange mollies, neon tetras, angelfish, flexing their fins, wriggling their slick bodies, doing loop-de-loops in mid-air—knee level. I am surprised until I remember that the air here is damp enough for fish. Nobody has fed them for days. Guiltily, I start scooping them up in my hands, one at a time. I move from the hallway into the dorm room, pass the cheap college furniture, and force the fish back through the water's surface. I sprinkle in the food. Then I turn and notice the eight or two hundred other fish tanks in the room—all full of hungry, neglected fish. I set to work, with a sandwich bag of fish food in one hand. It doesn't have enough flakes to feed all these fish, but as I sprinkle it, I never seem to have any less. I am feeding platys and catfish and an entire tank of African cichlids, lunging at the food, barely missing my fingers with their teeth. They break free of the water to snatch the food from mid-air, and I guide them, gnashing at me, back in.

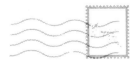

The Roles of the Game

My lawn chair is in the lake and so are my bare feet. July sun beats down on my hat. Palms upturned, breathing deeply, I am soaking up vitamin D and heat. A paperback novel lies uselessly closed in my lap. "You can't be a bunny." Both girls are behind me. One is mine, the other is a new friend from the playground. Mary from Maryland whom we met on the merry-go-round. (I can't make that stuff up. I don't even try.) "You can't be a bunny because you don't have the right shirt." They are playing little-girl-pretend in the sand behind me, in the shade of the poplars. Mary is not getting her way. In front of me, three older boys and a girl are tossing a football between them in the water. Submerged up to their chests, the boys flex and jockey. Their bent elbows form muscled angles with reflections of rippling biceps on the water's surface. "You really want to be a bunny, don't you?" The teenage girl brushes a strand of dark hair out of her eyes, squinting up at the chest of the boy. She giggles. He wants to show her how to throw the ball. He wants her to want to be shown. Her bikini top barely covers the essentials. She is showing plenty. Mary asks again, "Please?" One boy, the smallest one, misses the ball every time it comes his way. It thumps against the water, sending spray into his face. The girl giggles at that too, continually moving that same strand of hair, playing a big-girl-game. "Ok, fine. You can be a bunny."

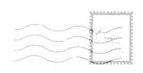

Shopping with Old People

Mid-day doctor's appointment and I'm the only one in the waiting room with brown hair. All other hairs are like angel hair or tinsel. Then to the supermarket for a few things, and the road between waiting room and produce department is clogged with my elders, driving slow, like they have all goddamned day. Turn down the aisle for some peanut butter, and it's blocked by someone driving her personal golf cart around the mid-day shipping boxes and pallets. The checkout lines are like the last chopper out of Saigon with only three registers open. I count my items—the number mercifully qualifies me for the express lane. Barely. (I would have put something back.) Outside, there's a jam-up at the cart corral—comfortable shoes shuffling behind wheeled baskets, and my breathing gets shallow and fast. Then this hunched-over woman, with her hand on the arm of her tall, gray husband moves slowly by me, on her way to their nondescript sedan. He moves as slowly as she does, and I imagine their grown children living somewhere in the world having no idea that their parents are at the supermarket, not worried at all about the jam-up. He moves like he has all day.

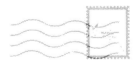

Celebration

We are by the edge of the bay, throwing rocks before jammies and teeth and stories and lights out. These first warm days of spring are an event here in New England. Such a long winter. Bare arms and toes tingling in the warmth as the feeling returns. My daughter hauls the heaviest rocks she can, carrying them low, between her knees, her back hunched over like a monkey. She hoists and jockeys, balances on the edge of the outcropping, and heaves them airborne. They fall into the rockweed and kelp below, not even reaching the water. My son throws pebbles, a fistful at a time, into the smooth evening water. Above, eleven different contrails are drawn on the blue of the sky, as flights from major cities on this seaboard, aim their radar toward Newfoundland where they will hang a right and make the crossing. People up there, sipping cocktails, asking for peanuts, trying to settle in for the discomfort of the night. Propping on small pillows and balled-up jackets. My son draws his arm back, pulls a handful of stones over his shoulder. "Want to see this celebration?" he asks, then lets loose. Stones land in unison, turning the calm water into patterns and weaves, circular ripples laying across one another like a rounded grid. The contrails become sine curves, become radio frequencies or heart rhythms, then flatten out as the water stills.

How To Visit Your Midwestern In-Laws

Don't admit to spending money. On anything. Know the price of gas in your town. Not just what it was the day you left, but the week before that. Maybe the month. Don't drink. Don't swear. Be ready for your cynical, east-coast jokes to be met with silence. Forget left and right, learn east from west. Check your overeating, overabundance-loving ways at baggage claim, and hope the airlines throw them out at 20,000 feet. You won't need them until you get home. Remember the rules for football—you learned them once. You can fake it. (Balls go up, and people make downs.) Prepare for stories that begin with the ending. Don't touch the thermostat. Don't buy anything new that could possibly be found used. Anywhere. Ever. Relax into small portions.

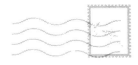

How to Go Bowling with Your Michigan Brother-in-Law

Don't mention the unions.

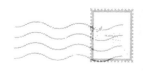

Kate and Al

It started with jars of pickles, she said. We stood, looking at her canvasses, where they leaned against the studio wall. *I started with jars of things I was canning from the garden—pickles, tomato sauce—I made still lifes of them, and that got me interested in glass.* Behind us, on shelves lining the walls like insulation, were decades and decades of glass. Bottles, glasses, glasses that used to be jam jars, vases, candy dishes. *And then I got interested in birds, so I started adding bird watching stuff.* From a beam running down the studio's center hung at least a dozen old bird cages. Gold, wooden, burnished metallic. The paintings included binoculars and Pederson guidebooks, nests surrounding pale blue eggs, feathers. *You're also interested in colour*, Al reminded her, moving himself onto a four-legged stool. The canvasses were huge—like the tops of large dinner tables. *Yes, yes. I really love colour, so I end up reaching for things to add colour.* Calico tablecloths, bouquets of bittersweet or Chinese lanterns, jellybeans, or M&Ms. Al is older, but contains newer parts. He got a new heart eighteen years ago, and then one of Kate's kidneys. I am in their home in Sterling Valley, seduced in place by the painterly brush strokes on her pieces and his in this studio he started before the transplant and finished months after. *You had help*, she had to remind him when he told me the story. *Well, yes. I had a student help me. But I supervised.* He left us in the studio while he took the dog out, and we didn't watch him leave. Our eyes were moving across the paintings still, taking in the edges of cloth and rounded, clear, red glass plates and blue vases and green drinking glasses with flowers around the lips. *People think it's hard to paint glass*, she said. *But it's really like anything else.*

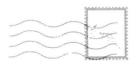

Larch

I take my kids for a walk down our dirt road because you and I are fighting and I need to move my muscles and get some air. It's early summer, and slender tamarack needles are green the way that new things are beautiful. By October, they will turn yellow and fall. The kids have too much energy pent up from nine months of school, just ended. I make them race and tag and jump. Keep them moving. Keep their feet shaking the ground. The rhythm of my legs and soles of my feet and the yardage passing under my body wear our fight into a smooth heaviness in my gut. A tension, like a bass string, like a standing wave. The kids find a rounded rock, the size and shape of a box turtle, broken cleanly into two pieces. They hurl the larger piece to the ground, and it cracks in two. All three parts reveal the same, dark core shaped like... a horse? A monster? A useless fight? We each pocket a piece of permanent rock under temporary green.

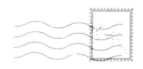

Catch 22

In the whitest part of the whitest state, a black man swims laps in the lane next to mine. How did he get here? And why would he bother? I make purposeful eye contact and smile too broadly, aiming for that sweet spot between friendly and crazy. He is muscular—a fast swimmer. My friend Charles says that black men like him exchange a certain glance when they meet each other; one that says, *"We didn't get shot or knifed in some stupid gang beef or overdose or wind up in the joint for the rest of our lives. We didn't catch a bullet from some hothead cop, or get our brains scrambled by his nightstick."* I want my smile to say something in between "Congratulations" and "I understand" and "I'm not that person." But I know that my skin, my puffy, doughy muscles, my slow swimming, my need for him to know that I'm different are the things that make me not different. It's a Joseph Heller book. We pass each other, facing for breath, then facing the bottom, the same chlorine finding its way around the rubber seals of our goggles. He is so dark that he seems like anti-matter against the false blue water, yet it buoys him as it lifts me; we slice at it with pointed fingers and cocked elbows. We meet at one end, stopping for a break between laps, supporting ourselves against the pebbly concrete. He smiles back.

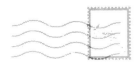

Herzog

A Chevy truck with "4X4" on the side panel sitting on someone's lawn, and I'm back in his living room. I looked for his blue truck everywhere I went the summer that I turned twenty. He was inappropriately too old for me, and he knew it, but I didn't. He was inappropriately chopping up parcels of land for sale too, and I knew it but he didn't. My father called him a carpet bagger and he treated our town like we were a third world country, there just for him. I invited him to a movie with me and my best friend, then asked her to stay home. He said, "You probably threatened her life," as I climbed into his truck cab. I pretended I didn't know what he was talking about. He taught me to drink vodka and grapefruit juice—a drink called a Greyhound. He loved Bellow. I was a Fitzgerald girl. Years after that, after I had switched to wine, after I had dated men my age, after I had stopped looking for his truck, after his real estate office was shuttered up, I found his name in ink inside the front cover of a paperback copy of <u>Herzog</u> in a box at a yard sale. I flipped it open to this phrase, "bone-breaking burden of selfhood," then paid a quarter for it. That paperback lives on my shelf, among my other volumes, among my other bone breaks.

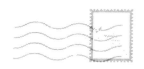

Lump in My Throat

I thought for days I was dying, that the lump would not be benign. I took to the hot safety of the shower, tried to swallow the lump, felt my way around it. It felt like words I couldn't quite get out. The size of a cigarette butt, it told me it wanted to limit my days, made me regret things I had done, the butts I had stamped out with my shoe on pavement. It wasn't cancer. I googled it, and it probably wasn't even there. Globus Pharyngeus—*frequently a symptom of depression.* I know this thing. This thing can fold me in half with its iron skillets dangling from twine tied to my arms. It's a rough voice through a red receiver held hard against my brain saying "drink more smoke more sleep less sleep more eat those, you'll feel better." Driving me around too fast without enough oil, not enough braking on the turns. Then submersing me in dark salt water, making the quilts too heavy to lift, the blinds too heavy to lift, my eyelids…the same, and I could sleep for days. It comes like fog and gauze and hangovers and power outages. Like a padded hammer on a gong. Like big words. Like a lump I can't crawl over.

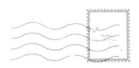

November 2011

Unseasonable warmth. Windows rolled down. "That is worth something when you think about it." Paul Simon pours from my dashboard. "That is worth some money." No jacket on, and that's really bad. Drumming on the wheel, full-on brass. "Summer skies, the stars are falling." Driving east, toward the coast to the sound of batà and tambourine. Thanksgiving's coming, and it feels wrong to plan cranberry sauce in short sleeves. Hunters have parked their trucks at random intervals along the road. Drivers, looking like fat traffic cones, sip coffee from thermoses. Ropes and bungee cords wait in truck beds. Can't track the deer with no snow. "This is the only life. Sorrow is everywhere you turn." Warm, salty, dangerous air rearranges my hair. Leaves are green and alive. Chimneys are cold. Rhythms are off. Unreasonable warmth. "And that is worth something when you think about it. That is worth some money."

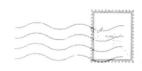

Seeing Red

The guy in the booth next to ours in the diner is sounding off about Obama coming for his guns while the small bodies are still cooling in Newtown. Maine can't decide what colour it is. Red in the Senate, blue in the House, whatever colour symbolizes the tea party (dishwater grey?) in the governor's office. I stop talking to you so I can listen to him, and your eyes tell me to stay out of it. He is afforded this space, while I am quietly folding and unfolding my napkin. Makes me want to dump dishwater on him. A grizzled Maine guy with suspenders holding his sagging jeans up over his gut—barely. His grimy baseball cap is set on the table next to him out of respect to us ladies. His scalp, likely exposed to too many days on the water, hauling in traps, cutting lines, is the colour of beet juice.

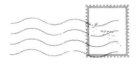

Ring of Fire

Chop it yourself, and it warms you twice. That's what they say, but firewood is too much damned work. It's enough that we have to carry it from the woodshed to the living room. I don't want to chop it myself too. Our firewood holder is round—like two steel hula hoops balanced on their sides—and when it's full, it holds a perfect circle of fuel. The work of lifting split pieces of birch and maple and balancing them in my arms reminds my back to remind me that I'm aging. Fast. But heat from a wood fire warms your bones first, so it's worth it. The stove is a magic trick, a fire blazing in the middle of the house. It's like living with a dragon. In the coldest months, we fill the wood holder once each week, and each time, the twelve round trips to the wood pile makes every inch of my spine crack, makes me crave a night in traction. Kara wants the firewood holder full. No, more than full. She wants it full with extra wood stacked on top. She wants it overfull, wants us to make it through the first day without spoiling the arc of the circle of wood that feels as impossible as having a fire at all. I play grasshopper to her ant and would sometimes rather half-fill it more often. But today, I made the twelfth trip from the woodshed with my lower back screaming in protest, making the effort to make her happy. This is not just what we do. It's who we are.

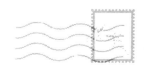

Racing

I am setting up the race track that my brother sent from Massachusetts. He sent two boxes of stuff his kids have outgrown. Legos. Playdough. A metal lunchbox. Some jackets. And an electric race track with two cars. My kids are hovering, pressing me, rummaging through the pieces of track, standing exactly where I need them not to. I'm trying to keep the area clear, give myself room to wrestle this thing into whatever shape it's supposed to be. (An oval? A figure eight? A circle? I can't figure it out.) The kids can't stay away. "What's this part? Where does this go? Are you done yet? When can we play with it?" The controls are gun-shaped and wired to the track. One piece has its connective tabs broken off, so I use electrical tape to secure it to the adjacent section. The kids are fighting now over who gets the blue car. Faster. It's a race. I plug it in and pull the trigger. There's no power.

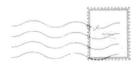

Woodcock

I know the difference between a spring peeper and a woodcock. I can tell the chirping from the buzzing. And I know when you're trying to use your optimism to change me, to hold back the season I'm always in. The woodcock wants sex, and he's out there in our driveway begging for it—buzzing and whirring—his wings in crazy upward flight. You're on the road—still—hard at your work, holding too many strings. I'm here, alone—buzzing and whirring—wanting you home. Peepers are babies, just growing their legs and webbed feet in the pond. I'm not a baby, but I can still act like one. I know it could always be worse, but I miss you. Cars break down, parts are backordered, then the wrong fucking one is delivered, you are stuck, and I am watching our limited time together dwindle while peepers and woodcocks begin and finish the work of the season. I know what you need from me over the phone line, between the cell towers, and across all those miles of highway between our house and that motel where you wait. I can be the woodcock, not the peeper. I can buzz you home.

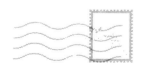

The And

My new cello teacher is a piano player, but I don't care because I believe that, on some level, he can unlock the cello's secrets anyway. I have taken lessons from cello players, but I find that I don't speak their language—like trying to learn Spanish from someone who doesn't speak any English. That takes a focused immersion that I frankly don't have time for. He agrees to take me on as a student, but seems skeptical. He listens to me play "Southwind," and notes that, in some measures, my rhythm is off. He tells me to play it the way I think it's supposed to really sound, and I don't know what he means. He uses a sharp pencil to point to the notes he's talking about, and he counts, "One, two *and* three *and* four." I sigh. "I don't understand that whole *and* thing." He stops the lesson to explain. The *and* is the space between the beats. The *and* holds time and rhythm and music in its three letters. The *and* is everything. The *and* is the lifespan of sound. And he spends an hour teaching me how to count to four.

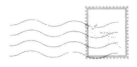

Cowaling

My kids don't believe me, but we're going to the farm to sing to the cows. "They love it," the farmer tells us. "It helps with milk production." We gather on Christmas Eve, a group eighteen strong, in the pungent barn—it is long with stalls and deep with odor. The cows are sideways chewing, looking at us with what I assume is interest. My daughter finds a friend, and they disappear between stacks of hay bales. My son is stuck with me. I stick a song sheet in his hand, but he is eight now and knows just enough to be too embarrassed to sing in front of people. Or cows. Especially cows. The farmer wears a Santa hat and faces us, ready to lead us through Jingle Bells and Silent Night. He's also wearing his farming clothes, neck-to-ankle Carhartts, and mucky boots. He's been up longer than the sun and will not lie down until long after dark. He feeds us, and if he wants us to sing, we will. Our voices mingle and rise like smoke. Most of us sing the right notes. The cows—caramel-coloured jerseys, mostly—munch hay while they regard our fleece-clad group. I do wonder what they think, while I nudge my son with my hip. "Sing," I urge him. "It's fun." He has googly, felt eyeballs hot glued onto his hat for fun, and so it's four eyes that glare at me in that "don't-talk-to-me" way. I whisper a reminder, "There's hot chocolate after." His glare falls to his boots, but he does not sing.

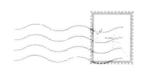

Winter 2015

It was the winter of bobcats and caterpillars. These huge machines, fitted with hydraulics and buckets—earth movers. Rock shifters. Smashers and relocaters. Diggers. The language of aliens and wildlife. One hundred inches of snow fell in three weeks, and the white landscape sprouted yellow and green machines, driven by men in chin-to-boots, insulated jumpsuits and woolly hats and gloves, their heads enveloped in clouds of frozen breath. US Route One south disappeared into an abrupt wall of snow where it passed through an open blueberry barren—the wind had urged the dry snow to drift wherever it felt it wanted more, more, more, and cars had to wait while an orange backhoe found the asphalt again, put the snow back in the margins. Conversations over hands huddling around cups of hot anything turned without cessation to shovels, roof rakes, snow blowers—the things we use to keep the driveway clear, the path to the woodpile, the route to the propane tank—the things we use to allow commerce and life to move. "Soon enough," the postmaster said to me after selling me some stamps, "we'll be complaining about the heat." Outside, an excavator, churning and grinding, reclaimed the edges of the parking lot. The air smelled like diesel.

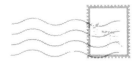

Wired for Fight

Thank god I don't actually have wings, or I would hover like a bee, bonking from flower to flower, from task to thing, from flight to fight. That moment when you trip and catch yourself before you actually fall—that tension, that so-close-to-smashing-my-face-on-the-sidewalk feeling—that's my condition. My hands, wrapped around a coffee cup, banging away at the keyboard, flicking ash off a smoke, are actually clenched into fists on the inside. I am ready to take you on, ready to punch my way out of that day's paper bag. Meds help, but it makes me more anxious to rely on them. Sometimes I drink instead. This feeling, like a burglar, shakes me awake in the night, grabs me by the shoulders, rocks me hard and shouts into my face, "You didn't check the battery in the smoke detector. You're murdering your kids," then it drops me in a pool of sweat and sleeplessness. When I trudge back to bed from checking the battery, it's still there. "Pay attention," it says, sitting at the foot of my bed. It has a knife. It's casually whittling a sharp stick. "I'm watching you." Last year, the cardiologist determined that the way my heart skips beats is just an electrical problem. "Nothing to worry about," he said before signing my discharge. "It's just your wiring."

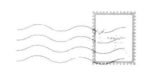

Bioluminescence

Kayaking well past bedtime, my son dangles his hand off starboard. His small fingers leave four trails of stars on the water's surface. Light drips from my paddle, just as it sparkles on the leading edge of our wake. The paddle leaves strokes of impossible diamonds, and our rudders give off sparks. It can't be that light is alive in this salty blackness, but it is. Dense fog lumbers across the bay, making the night a darker shade of black. We need light to find our way to the boat trailer, but it obscures the thing we came out to see. So we compromise and turn flashlights on and off, allowing our night vision to come and go, slowly bumping our way from landmark to landmark. From above, we must look like fluorescing microorganisms. My daughter's bow bumps into my port side, and I see her eyes wide with the surprise of yet another beautiful thing in the world.

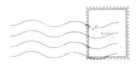

Amnio

I am a seal. A dolphin. A sea serpent. Through the stupidly teal, clear water, I see my son's skinny legs and his tight racing trunks. The surface, mirrored from below, cuts him off at the ribcage. He is in the shallow end, shooting baskets at a hoop suspended from the edge for the little kids. He sees me coming, moving like a shark, and meets me underwater. His face erupts in bubbles. They are jewels. Shards of mica. Drops of molten, white glass. Letting them stream behind him, he flicks flippered feet to get away from my outstretched fingers. His body curved like a comma, he evades. He is a diving shorebird. King Neptune. An electric eel. His cells still drift in the clear water of my body, and I think about when he floated in there, kicking, swimming, curving like punctuation. We break the surface, and he laughs at my efforts to catch him. Goggles adhere to his brow and cheekbones, leaving red marks, and droplets make their way down his shoulders and back. He has quickened. I will never capture him again.

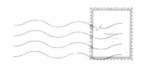

The End Begins

Bifocals. That's what she said to me. That it's time. My eyes have long been the only feature of this body that I love. My belly is too soft, too large. My hair can't decide anymore whether to be curly or straight. My face—too much like my brother's. But my eyes are sky, ocean, glaciers, cold river water. As she clicked the round lenses through the vision testing equipment—the thing that looks like an alien space mask—and had me choose which view was clearer, sharper, brighter, she said, "It's normal in your forties." Forty-three years of reading, driving, taking notes, being a witness. These eyes caress the curves of my lover, take in the growth of my children, and watch dying hurricanes whip the golden remnants of the garden each year. "You'll get used to them." Now when I lift my head to watch that early morning glow hit the tops of the trees and begin its walk down to the ground, it will have to be with raised eyes only, and my reading will be downcast through the lower part of the digitally-surfaced lens. It's normal for our bodies to start decaying before we're ready. We get used to it.

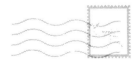

Acknowledgments

Writing takes place in solitude, but rewriting takes a committee. It's in the revision process that all the magic happens: it's where bad sentences get turned into something presentable, something you might want to share with a readership. Writers rarely attempt the daredevilry of publishing without a motley posse of scribblers, wordsmiths, and ink slingers who wield red pens like cattle prods. *Postcards* would still be a messy stack of papers on my desk if not for the help, encouragement, and occasional ego-wrecking smackdowns I received from my posse. Thanks go out to Rooze for riding herd on this entire project. (You were right about *Whitetail*.) More thanks to mentors Barbara Hurd and Debra Marquart for early encouragement and subsequent guidance. (You were both always right about everything.) Big, broad thanks to the Stonecoast MFA faculty, staff, and community of students who told me to me zip myself into the skin of a writer and wear it comfortably. (You were right. I can do this.)

Several of the pieces in this manuscript have appeared in other publications.

"Larch" appeared in *About Place Journal,* Volume II, Issue I, 2013

"Heat," "Hay Pond," "Herzog," "The And," "Bioluminescence," "I Didn't Miss You Until This Morning" and "Back from the Trip" appeared in *Exit 7: A Journal of Literature and Arts*, Spring 2014.

"Batboy is Disappointed" appeared in *Proximity Magazine,* July 2014.

"Marriage" and "Marriage Two" appeared in *Bluestem*, December 2015.

About the Author

Penny Guisinger lives and writes on the easternmost tip of the United States. In 2015, she had one essay named as a notable in Best American Essays and another nominated for a Pushcart Prize. Other work has appeared in *Fourth Genre, River Teeth, The Rumpus, Guernica, Solstice Literary Magazine, Under the Gum Tree*, multiple anthologies, and other places. She is an Assistant Editor at Brevity, the founding organizer of *Iota: Short Prose Conference*, and a graduate of the Stonecoast MFA Program. She lives with her wife and kids, two dogs, two leopard geckos, and a constantly changing number of tropical fish. She can be found at *pennyguisinger.com*.

Vine Leaves Literary Journal

What We Want

The written vignette:

"Vignette" is a word that originally meant "something that may be written on a vine leaf." It's a snapshot in words. It differs from flash fiction or a short story in that its aim does not lie within the realms of traditional structure or plot. The vignette focuses on one element, mood, character, setting or object. It's descriptive, excellent for character or theme exploration and wordplay. Through a vignette, you create an atmosphere.

A vignette can be written in a variety of forms.

We're looking for:

prose ❖ poetry ❖ script

We will accept all genres except erotica. Write something brilliant and woo us into publishing it!

The visual vignette:

Artwork or photography will be considered for the cover and interior of each issue. Send us a piece of work you believe represents a slice of life.

When to Submit

Submissions are open all year round.
We publish biannually online and in print.

To be published in our MAY ISSUE, submit between September 1st – February 28th.

To be published in our NOVEMBER ISSUE, submit between March 1st – August 31st.

Visit our website for further guidelines:
vineleavesliteraryjournal.com

Payment

We pay $5 AUD per acceptance into the journal. This means if we accept 1 poem, you'll get $5. If we accept three pieces of prose, you'll get $5. If we accept two poems and three prose and one photo, you'll get $5. At the moment we can only issue payment via PayPal. OR, you can receive a contributor copy of the print journal instead of payment.

Vine Leaves Literary Journal — © 2011—2015
Australia & Greece
Online ISSN: 2202-2767 — Print ISSN: 2204-4574
Vine Leaves Press — Australia & Greece
ABN: 39159817423
All staff are volunteers.
vineleaves.editors@gmail.com

The Annual Vine Leaves Vignette Collection Award

Submissions open: June 1 – February 28.

Includes a cash prize of $500 (USD), publication by Vine Leaves Press (paperback and eBook), 20 copies of the paperback, worldwide distribution, and promotion through *Vine Leaves Literary Journal* and staff websites. Author will receive a 70% net royalty on all eBook and print sales.

Visit *vineleavesliteraryjournal.com/vine-leaves-vignette -collection-award* for details.

Ⅵ **Please visit *vineleavesliteraryjournal.com* for submission guidelines.**

www.vineleavesliteraryjournal.com/donate

Vine Leaves Literary Journal now tallies more than 4000 unique views a month and the compliments we've been receiving by email make this job worth every second of effort.

This is thanks to YOU. Without your brilliant poetry, prose and art, this journal would not exist.

But the more we grow, the more we start to scrape the bottom of the money barrel. Especially since we are now publishing single-author vignette collections through Vine Leaves Press in both paperback and eBook. But this means any money that we receive goes straight back into the journal and paying contributors for their work.

Our piggy bank is always on the brink of empty. We have tried to acquire grant support through the Australian Council for the Arts, but in order to be eligible, we have to publish only Australian literature.

We are not willing to do that. There is a *world* of amazing writers out there!

Can you help us?

Please do us the honour of donating a few bucks to our mission: to give the vignette, a forgotten literary form, the exposure and credit it deserves.

Just think of it as buying two coffees one morning, instead of one, for the greater good of the vignette!

Thanks,
The Vine Leaves Team

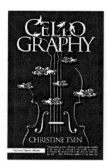

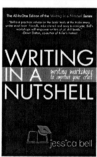

Vine Leaves Literary Journal was founded to offer the vignette, a forgotten literary form, the exposure and credit it deserves.

The journal, published quarterly online, is a lush synergy of atmospheric prose, poetry, photography and illustrations, put together with an eye for aesthetics as well as literary merit. The annual print anthology showcases the very best pieces from throughout the year.

Each vignette merges to create a vivid snapshot in time and place. Prepare for big stories in small spaces, between and beyond the words.

Read one at a time.

Taste them. Savour them.

Live them.

www.vineleavesliteraryjournal.com